A WITNESS AND A WARNING

A Modern-day Prophet
Testifies of the Book of Mormon

EZRA TAFT BENSON

Deseret Book Company
Salt Lake City, Utah

No part of this book may be reproduced in any
form or by any means·without permission in writing
from the publisher, Deseret Book Company,
P.O. Box 30178, Salt Lake City, Utah 84130.
Deseret Book is a registered trademark of
Deseret Book Company.

First printing April 1988
Second printing July 1988

Library of Congress Catalog Card Number 88-70533
ISBN 0-87579-153-0

Contents

Foreword

My beloved brethren and sisters:

Sister Benson and I have a great love for the Book of Mormon and we try to read it every day.

The Book of Mormon is the instrument that God has designed to "sweep the earth as with a flood, to gather out His elect unto the New Jerusalem." (Moses 7:62.)

This sacred volume of scripture has not been, nor is it yet, central in our preaching, our teaching, and our missionary work. We have not adequately used "the most correct of any book on earth."

Presently the Book of Mormon is studied in our Sunday School and seminary classes every fourth year. This four-year pattern, however, must *not* be followed by Church members in their personal study of the standard works. All scripture is not of equal value. The book that is the "keystone of our religion" and that will get a man "nearer to God by abiding by its precepts, than by any other book" needs to be studied constantly. (*History of the Church* 4:461.)

In section 84 of the Doctrine and Covenants, the Lord declares that the whole Church and all the children of Zion are under condemnation because of the way we have treated the Book of Mormon. (Verses 54-58.) This condemnation has not been lifted, nor will it be until we repent.

The Lord states that we must not only *say* but we must *do*. We have neither said enough nor have we done enough with this divine instrument—the key to conversion. As a result, as individuals, as families, and as the Church, we sometimes have felt the scourge and judgment God said would be "poured out upon the children of Zion" because of our neglect of this book.

The Lord inspired His servant Lorenzo Snow to reemphasize the principle of tithing to redeem the Church from financial bondage. In those days the General Authorities took that message to the members of the Church. So too in our day the Lord has inspired His servant to reemphasize the Book of Mormon to get the Church out from under condemnation—the scourge and judgment.

We invite each member of the Church to read again and again the Book of Mormon. Those who teach or speak in Church meetings should carefully and prayerfully use the Book of Mormon to strengthen and enhance their messages and presentations.

I bless you with increased *understanding* of the Book of Mormon. I promise you that from this moment forward, if we will daily sup from its pages and abide by its precepts, God will pour out upon each child of Zion and the Church a blessing hitherto unknown—and we will plead to the Lord that He will begin to lift the condemnation—the scourge and judgment. Of this I bear solemn witness.

I promise you that as you more diligently study modern revelation on gospel subjects, your power to teach and preach will be magnified and you will so move the cause of Zion that added numbers will enter into the house of the Lord as well as the mission field.

Foreword

I bless you with increased desire to flood the earth with the Book of Mormon, to gather out from the world the elect of God who are yearning for the truth but know not where to find it.

Faithfully your brother,

Ezra Taft Benson

Chapter 1

The Book of Mormon
Is the Word of God

As members of The Church of Jesus Christ of Latter-day Saints, "We believe . . . the Book of Mormon to be the word of God." (Eighth Article of Faith.) God has so declared it, so have its writers, so have its witnesses, and so do all those who have read it and received a personal revelation from God as to its truthfulness.

In section 20 of the Doctrine and Covenants the Lord says that he gave Joseph Smith "power from on high . . . to translate the Book of Mormon; which contains . . . the fulness of the gospel of Jesus Christ . . . which was given by inspiration." (Verses 8–10.)

Nephi, one of the prophet-writers of the Book of Mormon, testifies that the book contains "the words of Christ" (2 Nephi 33:10), and Moroni, the last writer in the book, testifies that "these things are true" (Moroni 7:35).

This same Moroni, as an angelic being sent from God, showed these ancient records to three witnesses in our day. Their testimony of the records is contained in the front of the Book of Mormon. They state: "We also know that they have been translated by the gift and power of

God, for his voice hath declared it unto us; wherefore we know of a surety that the work is true."

And Joseph Smith, the Prophet, the instrument whom God used to translate this record, testified that "the Book of Mormon was the most correct of any book on earth, and the keystone of our religion, and a man would get nearer to God by abiding by its precepts, than by any other book." (*History of the Church* 4:461.)

The Book of Mormon was written for us today. God is the author of the book. It is a record of a fallen people, compiled by inspired men for our blessing today. Those people never had the book — it was meant for us. Mormon, the ancient prophet after whom the book is named, abridged centuries of records. God, who knows the end from the beginning, told him what to include in his abridgment that we would need for our day. Mormon turned the records over to his son Moroni, the last recorder; and Moroni, writing over 1,500 years ago but speaking to us today, states: "Behold, I speak unto you as if ye were present, and yet ye are not. But behold, Jesus Christ hath shown you unto me, and I know your doing." (Mormon 8:35.)

The purpose of the Book of Mormon is stated on the title page. It is "to the convincing of the Jew and Gentile that Jesus is the Christ, the Eternal God."

Nephi, the first prophet-writer in the Book of Mormon, states: "For the fulness of mine intent is that I may persuade men to come unto the God of Abraham, and the God of Isaac, and the God of Jacob, and be saved.

"Wherefore, the things which are pleasing unto the world I do not write, but the things which are pleasing unto God and unto those who are not of the world.

"Wherefore, I shall give commandment unto my seed, that they shall not occupy these plates with things which

2

are not of worth unto the children of men." (1 Nephi 6:4–6.)

The Book of Mormon brings men to Christ through two basic means. First, it tells in a plain manner of Christ and His gospel. It testifies of His divinity and of the necessity for a Redeemer and the need of our putting trust in Him. It bears witness of the Fall and the Atonement and the first principles of the gospel, including our need of a broken heart and a contrite spirit and a spiritual rebirth. It proclaims we must endure to the end in righteousness and live the moral life of a Saint.

Second, the Book of Mormon exposes the enemies of Christ. It confounds false doctrines and lays down contention. (See 2 Nephi 3:12.) It fortifies the humble followers of Christ against the evil designs, strategies, and doctrines of the devil in our day. The type of apostates in the Book of Mormon is similar to the type we have today. God, with his infinite foreknowledge, so molded the Book of Mormon that we might see the error and know how to combat false educational, political, religious, and philosophical concepts of our time.

Now God expects us to use the Book of Mormon in several ways. We are to read it ourselves—carefully, prayerfully—and ponder as we read, as to whether this book is the work of God or of an unlearned youth. And then when we are finished reading the things in the book, Moroni exhorts us to put them to the test in these words:

"And when ye shall receive these things, I would exhort you that ye would ask God, the Eternal Father, in the name of Christ, if these things are not true; and if ye shall ask with a sincere heart, with real intent, having faith in Christ, he will manifest the truth of it unto you, by the power of the Holy Ghost." (Moroni 10:4.) I have done as

Moroni exhorts, and I can testify to you that this book is from God and so is verily true.

We are to use the Book of Mormon as the basis for our teaching. In section 42 of the Doctrine and Covenants, the Lord states: "And again, the elders, priests and teachers of this church shall teach the principles of my gospel, which are in . . . the Book of Mormon, in the which is the fulness of the gospel." (Verse 12.)

As we read and teach, we are to liken the Book of Mormon scriptures unto us "that it might be for our profit and learning." (1 Nephi 19:23.)

We are to use the Book of Mormon in handling objections to the Church. God the Father and His Son Jesus Christ revealed themselves to Joseph Smith in a marvelous vision. After that glorious event, Joseph Smith told a minister about it. Joseph was surprised to hear the minister say that there were no such things as visions or revelations in these days, that all such things had ceased. (See Joseph Smith–History 1:21.)

This remark symbolizes practically all of the objections that have ever been made against the Church by non-members and dissident members alike. Namely, they do not believe that God reveals His will today to the Church through prophets of God. All objections, whether they be on abortion, plural marriage, seventh-day worship, etc., basically hinge on whether Joseph Smith and his successors were and are prophets of God receiving divine revelation. Here, then, is a procedure to handle most objections through the use of the Book of Mormon.

First, understand the objection.

Second, give the answer from revelation.

Third, show how the correctness of the answer really depends on whether or not we have modern revelation through modern prophets.

Fourth, explain that whether or not we have modern prophets and revelation really depends on whether the Book of Mormon is true.

Therefore, the only problem the objector has to resolve for himself is whether the Book of Mormon is true. For if the Book of Mormon is true, then Jesus is the Christ, Joseph Smith was his prophet, The Church of Jesus Christ of Latter-day Saints is true, and it is being led today by a prophet receiving revelation.

Our main task is to declare the gospel and do it effectively. We are not obligated to answer every objection. Every man eventually is backed up to the wall of faith, and there he must make his stand. "And if they are not the words of Christ, judge ye," said Nephi, "for Christ will show unto you, with power and great glory, that they are his words, at the last day; and you and I shall stand face to face before his bar; and ye shall know that I have been commanded of him to write these things." (2 Nephi 33:11.) Every man must judge for himself, knowing God will hold him accountable.

The Book of Mormon is to be used "for a standard unto my people, which are of the house of Israel," the Lord says, and its words "shall hiss forth unto the ends of the earth." (2 Nephi 29:2.) We, the members of the Church, and particularly the missionaries, have to be the "hissers," or the tellers and testifiers, of the Book of Mormon unto the ends of the earth.

The Book of Mormon is the great standard we are to use. It shows that Joseph Smith was a prophet. It contains the words of Christ, and its great mission is to bring men to Christ and all other things are secondary. The golden question of the Book of Mormon is, "Do you want to learn more of Christ?" The Book of Mormon is the great finder of the golden contact. It does not contain things which are "pleasing unto the world" (1 Nephi 6:5), and so the worldly are not interested in it. It is a great sieve.

Anyone who has diligently sought to know the doctrines and teachings of the Book of Mormon and has used it conscientiously in missionary work knows within his soul that this is the instrument which God has given to the missionaries to convince the Jew and Gentile and Lamanite of the truthfulness of our message.

Now, we have not been using the Book of Mormon as we should. Our homes are not as strong unless we are using it to bring our children to Christ. Our families may be corrupted by worldly trends and teachings unless we know how to use the book to expose and combat the falsehoods in socialism, organic evolution, rationalism, humanism, and so forth. Our missionaries are not as effective unless they are "hissing forth" with it. Social, ethical, cultural, or educational converts will not survive under the heat of the day unless their taproots go down to the fulness of the gospel which the Book of Mormon contains. Our Church classes are not as spirit-filled unless we hold it up as a standard. And our nation will continue to degenerate unless we read and heed the words of the God of this land, Jesus Christ, and quit building up and upholding the secret combinations which the Book of Mormon tells us proved the downfall of both previous American civilizations.

Some of the early missionaries, on returning home, were reproved by the Lord in section 84 of the Doctrine and Covenants because they had treated lightly the Book of Mormon. As a result, their minds had been darkened. The Lord said that this kind of treatment of the Book of Mormon brought the whole Church under condemnation, even all of the children of Zion. And then the Lord said, "And they shall remain under this condemnation until they repent and remember the new covenant, even the Book of Mormon." (See verses 54–57.) Are we still under that condemnation?

Reading the Book of Mormon is one of the greatest persuaders to get men on missions. We need more missionaries. But we also need better-prepared missionaries coming out of the wards and branches and homes where they know and love the Book of Mormon. A great challenge and day of preparation is at hand for missionaries to meet and teach with the Book of Mormon. We need missionaries to match our message.

And now grave consequences hang on our response to the Book of Mormon. "Those who receive it," said the Lord, "in faith, and work righteousness, shall receive a crown of eternal life;

"But those who harden their hearts in unbelief, and reject it, it shall turn to their own condemnation—

"For the Lord God has spoken it." (D&C 20:14–16.)

Is the Book of Mormon true? Yes.

Whom is it for? Us.

What is its purpose? To bring men to Christ.

How does it do this? By testifying of Christ and revealing His enemies.

How are we to use it? We are to get a testimony of it, we are to teach from it, we are to hold it up as a standard and "hiss it forth."

Have we been doing this? Not as we should, nor as we must.

Do eternal consequences rest upon our response to this book? Yes, either to our blessing or our condemnation.

Every Latter-day Saint should make the study of this book a lifetime pursuit. Otherwise he is placing his soul in jeopardy and neglecting that which could give spiritual and intellectual unity to his whole life. There is a difference between a convert who is built on the rock of Christ through the Book of Mormon and stays hold of that iron rod, and one who is not.

Over a quarter of a century ago I listened in the Tabernacle to these words: "A few years ago as I began to practice law, members of my family were a little uneasy. They were afraid I would lose my faith. I wanted to practice law, but I had an even greater desire to keep my testimony, and so I decided upon a little procedure which I recommend to you. For thirty minutes each morning before I began the day's work I read from the Book of Mormon . . . and in just a few minutes a day I read the Book of Mormon through, every year, for nine years. I know that it kept me in harmony, so far as I did keep in harmony, with the Spirit of the Lord. . . . [I]t will hold us as close to the Spirit of the Lord as anything I know." (See *Conference Report*, April 1949, pp. 36, 41.) That was President Marion G. Romney. I echo his counsel.

What, then, are we to say of the Book of Mormon? I bear witness that it is verily true. I know this as I know that I live. We stand with the Prophet Joseph Smith when he said, "I told the brethren that the Book of Mormon was the most correct of any book on earth, and the keystone of our religion, and a man would get nearer to God by abiding by its precepts, than by any other book."

May we know and use the keystone and get nearer to God.

Chapter 2

A New Witness for Christ

For some years now I have been deeply concerned that we are not using the Book of Mormon as God intends.

As I participated in the Mexico City Temple dedication, I received the distinct impression that God is not pleased with our neglect of the Book of Mormon.

In the eighty-fourth section of the Doctrine and Covenants, the Lord decreed that the whole Church was under condemnation, even all the children of Zion, because of the way they treated the Book of Mormon. Zion cannot fully arise and put on her beautiful garments if she is under this condemnation. (See D&C 82:14.)

How important is the Book of Mormon? Joseph Smith called it "the keystone of our religion." "Take away the Book of Mormon and the revelations," he said, "and where is our religion? We have none." (*History of the Church* 2:52.)

"This generation," said the Lord to Joseph Smith, the translator, "shall have my word through you." (D&C 5:10.) And so it has.

What is the major purpose of the Book of Mormon? To bring men to Christ and to be reconciled to Him, and

9

then to join His church — in that order. (See 2 Nephi 25:23; D&C 20:11–14, 35–37.)

The Lord instructed that the Book of Mormon proves that "God does inspire men and call them to his holy work in this age and generation, as well as in generations of old." (D&C 20:11.)

The Book of Mormon being true, then God did inspire His prophet Joseph Smith to translate it and did call him to do the holy work of restoring His church, even The Church of Jesus Christ of Latter-day Saints.

How are we to use the book?

We must first read it and gain a testimony for ourselves. Men may deceive each other, but God does not deceive men. Therefore, the Book of Mormon sets forth the best test for determining its truthfulness — namely, read it and then ask God if it is true.

Moroni, in the book's final chapter, issued that divine challenge to every reader. (Moroni 10:4.)

This, then, is the supreme assurance for the honest in heart — to know by personal revelation from God that the Book of Mormon is true. Millions have put it to that test and know, and increasing millions will yet know.

Now the spirit, as well as the body, is in need of constant nourishment. Yesterday's meal is not enough to sustain today's needs. So also an infrequent reading of "the most correct of any book on earth," as Joseph Smith called it, is not enough.

Not all truths are of equal value, nor are all scriptures of the same worth. What better way to nourish the spirit than to frequently feast from the book which the Prophet Joseph said would get a man "nearer to God by abiding by its precepts, than by any other book"?

The Book of Mormon is to be "a standard unto my

people, which are of the house of Israel," said the Lord. (2 Nephi 29:2.) It is a standard we should heed and follow.

In the twentieth section of the Doctrine and Covenants, the Lord devotes several verses to summarizing the vital truths which the Book of Mormon teaches. (See verses 17–36.) It speaks of God, the creation of man, the Fall, the Atonement, the ascension of Christ into heaven, prophets, faith, repentance, baptism, the Holy Ghost, endurance, prayer, justification and sanctification through grace, and loving and serving God.

We must know these essential truths. Aaron and Ammon and their brethren in the Book of Mormon taught these same kinds of truths to the Lamanite people (see Alma 18:22–39), who were "in the darkest abyss" (Alma 26:3). After accepting these eternal truths, the Book of Mormon states, those converted Lamanites never did fall away. (See Alma 23:6.)

If our children and grandchildren are taught and heed these same truths, will they fall away? We best instruct them in the Book of Mormon at our dinner table, by our firesides, at their bedsides, and in our letters and phone calls — in all of our goings and comings.

Some spiritually alert parents hold early-morning devotionals with their families in their homes. They have a hymn, prayer, and then read and discuss the Book of Mormon.

The Book of Mormon is for both member and nonmember. Combined with the Spirit of the Lord, the Book of Mormon is the greatest single tool which God has given us to convert the world. If we are to have the harvest of souls that He expects, then we must use the instrument which God has designed for that task — the Book of Mormon.

Elder Bruce R. McConkie stated, "Men can get nearer

to the Lord, can have more of the spirit of conversion and conformity in their hearts, can have stronger testimonies, and can gain a better understanding of the doctrines of salvation through the Book of Mormon than they can through the Bible.... There will be more people saved in the kingdom of God — ten thousand times over — because of the Book of Mormon than there will be because of the Bible." (Address at Book of Mormon Symposium, Brigham Young University, 18 August 1978.)

The Christian world has the Bible — and so do we. The Bible speaks of a people, the Jews; their land, the Holy Land; their prophets; and the birth and ministry of Jesus Christ.

But was there only one tribe of Israel? What of Joseph, the birthright son, who saved all of Israel's family from famine? What of Joseph, whose sons Israel blessed and said, "Let my name be named on them, and the name of my fathers Abraham and Isaac"? (Genesis 48:16.) What of Joseph, whom Israel blessed and promised that he would be "a fruitful bough by a well; whose branches run over the wall"? (Genesis 49:22.) Where is the record of Joseph?

We testify to the world that we have the record of Joseph — even the Book of Mormon. Like Judah, Joseph had a people — the Nephites and Lamanites. Like Judah, Joseph had prophets, and his descendants also had a visitation from Jesus Christ, even the resurrected Lord.

"Know ye not," the Lord says in the Book of Mormon, "that there are more nations than one? ...

" ... Know ye not that the testimony of two nations is a witness unto you that I am God, that I remember one nation like unto another?

" ... And because that I have spoken one word ye need not suppose that I cannot speak another." (2 Nephi 29:7–9.)

We invite all men everywhere to read the Book of Mormon, another testament of Jesus Christ.

The Bible sits on the pulpit of hundreds of different religious sects. The Book of Mormon, the record of Joseph, verifies and clarifies the Bible. It removes stumbling blocks, it restores many plain and precious things. We testify that when used together, the Bible and the Book of Mormon confound false doctrines, lay down contentions, and establish peace. (See 2 Nephi 3:12.)

We do not have to prove the Book of Mormon is true. The book is its own proof. All we need to do is read it and declare it. The Book of Mormon is not on trial—the people of the world, including the members of the Church, are on trial as to what they will do with this second witness for Christ.

I testify that the Book of Mormon is the word of God; and therefore Jesus is the Christ, Joseph Smith is a prophet, The Church of Jesus Christ of Latter-day Saints is true, with its authorized servants to perform the ordinances of salvation today.

Chapter 3

The Keystone
of Our Religion

I would like to discuss one of the most significant gifts given to the world in modern times. The gift I am thinking of is more important than any of the inventions and technological revolutions. This is a gift of greater value to mankind than even the many wonderful advances we have seen in modern medicine. It is of greater worth to mankind than the development of flight or space travel. I speak of the gift of the Book of Mormon.

This gift was prepared by the hand of the Lord over a period of more than a thousand years, then hidden up by him so that it would be preserved in its purity for our generation. Perhaps there is nothing that testifies more clearly of the importance of this modern book of scripture than what the Lord Himself has said about it.

By His own mouth He has borne witness (1) that it is true (D&C 17:6), (2) that it contains the truth of His words (D&C 19:26), (3) that it was translated by power from on high (D&C 20:8), (4) that it contains the fulness of the gospel of Jesus Christ (D&C 20:9; 42:12), (5) that it was given by inspiration and confirmed by the minis-

15

tering of angels (D&C 20:10), (6) that it gives evidence that the holy scriptures are true (D&C 20:11), and (7) that those who receive it in faith shall receive eternal life (D&C 20:14).

A second powerful testimony to the importance of the Book of Mormon is to note where the Lord placed its coming forth in the timetable of the unfolding Restoration. The only thing that preceded it was the First Vision. In that marvelous manifestation, the Prophet Joseph Smith learned the true nature of God and that God had a work for him to do. The coming forth of the Book of Mormon was the next thing to follow.

Think of that in terms of what it implies. The coming forth of the Book of Mormon preceded the restoration of the priesthood. It was published just a few days before the Church was organized. The Saints were given the Book of Mormon to read before they were given the revelations outlining such great doctrines as the three degrees of glory, celestial marriage, or work for the dead. It came before priesthood quorums and Church organization. Doesn't this tell us something about how the Lord views this sacred work?

Once we realize how the Lord feels about this book, it should not surprise us that He also gives us solemn warnings about how we receive it. After indicating that those who receive the Book of Mormon with faith, working righteousness, will receive a crown of eternal glory (see D&C 20:14), the Lord follows with this warning: "But those who harden their hearts in unbelief, and reject it, it shall turn to their own condemnation." (D&C 20:15.)

In 1829, the Lord warned the Saints that they are not to trifle with sacred things. (See D&C 6:12.) Surely the Book of Mormon is a sacred thing, and yet many trifle with it, or in other words, take it lightly, treat it as though it is of little importance.

In 1832, as some early missionaries returned from their fields of labor, the Lord reproved them for treating the Book of Mormon lightly. As a result of that attitude, He said, their minds had been darkened. Not only had treating this sacred book lightly brought a loss of light to themselves, it had also brought the whole Church under condemnation, even all the children of Zion. And then the Lord said, "And they shall remain under this condemnation until they repent and remember the new covenant, even the Book of Mormon." (D&C 84:54–57.)

Has the fact that we have had the Book of Mormon with us for over a century and a half made it seem less significant to us today? Do we remember the new covenant, even the Book of Mormon? In the Bible we have the Old Testament and the New Testament. The word *testament* is the English rendering of a Greek word that can also be translated as *covenant.* Is this what the Lord meant when He called the Book of Mormon the "new covenant"? It is indeed another testament or witness of Jesus. This is one of the reasons why we have recently added the words *Another Testament of Jesus Christ* to the title of the Book of Mormon.

If the early Saints were rebuked for treating the Book of Mormon lightly, are we under any less condemnation if we do the same?

There are three great reasons why Latter-day Saints should make the study of the Book of Mormon a lifetime pursuit.

The *first* is that the Book of Mormon is the keystone of our religion. This was the Prophet Joseph Smith's statement. He testified that "the Book of Mormon was the most correct of any book on earth, and the keystone of our religion." A keystone is the central stone in an arch. It holds all the other stones in place, and if removed, the arch crumbles.

There are three ways in which the Book of Mormon is the keystone of our religion. It is the keystone in our witness of Christ. It is the keystone of our doctrine. It is the keystone of testimony.

The Book of Mormon is the keystone in our witness of Jesus Christ, who is Himself the cornerstone of everything we do. It bears witness of His reality with power and clarity. Unlike the Bible, which passed through generations of copyists, translators, and corrupt religionists who tampered with the text, the Book of Mormon came from writer to reader in just one inspired step of translation. Therefore, its testimony of the Master is clear, undiluted, and full of power. But it does even more. Much of the Christian world today rejects the divinity of the Savior. They question His miraculous birth, His perfect life, and the reality of His glorious resurrection. The Book of Mormon teaches in plain and unmistakable terms about the truth of all of those. It also provides the most complete explanation of the doctrine of the Atonement. Truly, this divinely inspired book is a keystone in bearing witness to the world that Jesus is the Christ. (See title page of the Book of Mormon.)

The Book of Mormon is also the keystone of the doctrine of the resurrection. As mentioned before, the Lord Himself has stated that the Book of Mormon contains the "fulness of the gospel of Jesus Christ." (D&C 20:9.) That does not mean it contains every teaching, every doctrine ever revealed. Rather, it means that in the Book of Mormon we will find the fulness of those doctrines required for our salvation. And they are taught plainly and simply so that even children can learn the ways of salvation and exaltation. The Book of Mormon offers so much that broadens our understandings of the doctrines of salvation. Without it, much of what is taught in other scriptures would not be nearly so plain and precious.

Finally, the Book of Mormon is the keystone of testimony. Just as the arch crumbles if the keystone is removed, so does all the Church stand or fall with the truthfulness of the Book of Mormon. The enemies of the Church understand this clearly. This is why they go to such great lengths to try to disprove the Book of Mormon, for if it can be discredited, the Prophet Joseph Smith goes with it. So does our claim to priesthood keys, and revelation, and the restored Church. But in like manner, if the Book of Mormon be true—and millions have now testified that they have the witness of the Spirit that it is indeed true—then one must accept the claims of the Restoration and all that accompanies it.

Yes, the Book of Mormon is the keystone of our religion—the keystone of our testimony, the keystone of our doctrine, and the keystone in the witness of our Lord and Savior.

The *second* great reason why we must make the Book of Mormon a center focus of study is that it was written for our day. The Nephites never had the book; neither did the Lamanites of ancient times. It was meant for us. Mormon wrote near the end of the Nephite civilization. Under the inspiration of God, who sees all things from the beginning, he abridged centuries of records, choosing the stories, speeches, and events that would be most helpful to us.

Each of the major writers of the Book of Mormon testified that he wrote for future generations. Nephi said: "The Lord God promised unto me that these things which I write shall be kept and preserved, and handed down

19

unto my seed, from generation to generation." (2 Nephi 25:21.) His brother Jacob, who succeeded him, wrote similar words: "For [Nephi] said that the history of his people should be engraven upon his other plates, and that I should preserve these plates and hand them down unto my seed, from generation to generation." (Jacob 1:3.) Enos and Jarom both indicated that they too were writing not for their own people but for future generations. (See Enos 1:15–16; Jarom 1:2.)

Mormon himself said, "Yea, I speak unto you, ye remnant of the house of Israel." (Mormon 7:1.) And Moroni, the last of the inspired writers, actually saw our day and time. "Behold," he said, "the Lord hath shown unto me great and marvelous things concerning that which must shortly come, at that day when these things shall come forth among you.

"Behold, I speak unto you as if ye were present, and yet ye are not. But behold, Jesus Christ hath shown you unto me, and I know your doing." (Mormon 8:34–35.)

If they saw our day, and chose those things which would be of greatest worth to us, is not that how we should study the Book of Mormon? We should constantly ask ourselves, "Why did the Lord inspire Mormon (or Moroni or Alma) to include that in his record? What lesson can I learn from that to help me live in this day and age?"

And there is example after example of how that question will be answered. For example, in the Book of Mormon we find a pattern for preparing for the Second Coming. A major portion of the book centers on the few decades just prior to Christ's coming to America. By careful study of that time period, we can determine why some were destroyed in the terrible judgments that preceded His coming and what brought others to stand at the temple in the land of Bountiful and thrust their hands into the wounds of His hands and feet.

From the Book of Mormon we learn how disciples of Christ live in times of war. From the Book of Mormon we see the evils of secret combinations portrayed in graphic and chilling reality. In the Book of Mormon we find lessons for dealing with persecution and apostasy. We learn much about how to do missionary work. And more than anywhere else, we see in the Book of Mormon the dangers of materialism and setting our hearts on the things of the world. Can anyone doubt that this book was meant for us and that in it we find great power, great comfort, and great protection?

The *third* reason that the Book of Mormon is of such value to Latter-day Saints is given in the same statement by the Prophet Joseph Smith cited previously. He said, "I told the brethren that the Book of Mormon was the most correct of any book on earth, and the keystone of our religion, and a man would get nearer to God by abiding by its precepts, than by any other book." That is the third reason for studying the book. It helps us draw nearer to God. Is there not something deep in our hearts that longs to draw nearer to God, to be more like Him in our daily walk, to feel His presence with us constantly? If so, then the Book of Mormon will help us do so more than any other book.

It is not just that the Book of Mormon teaches us truth, though it indeed does that. It is not just that the Book of Mormon bears testimony of Christ, though it indeed does that, too. But there is something more. There is a power in the book which will begin to flow into your lives the moment you begin a serious study of the book. You will find greater power to resist temptation. You will find the power to avoid deception. You will find the power to stay on the strait and narrow path. The scriptures are called "the words of life" (see D&C 84:85), and nowhere is that more true than it is of the Book of Mormon. When you begin to hunger and thirst after those words, you will find life in greater and greater abundance.

I implore you with all my heart that you consider with great solemnity the importance of the Book of Mormon to you personally and to the Church collectively.

Let us not remain under condemnation, with its scourge and judgment, by treating lightly this great and marvelous gift the Lord has given to us. Rather, let us win the promises associated with treasuring it up in our hearts. (D&C 84:54–58.)

I have received many letters from Saints, both young and old, from all over the world who have accepted the challenge to read and study the Book of Mormon.

I have been thrilled by their accounts of how their lives have been changed and how they have drawn closer to the Lord as a result of their commitment. These glorious testimonies have reaffirmed to my soul the words of the Prophet Joseph Smith that the Book of Mormon is truly "the keystone of our religion" and that a man and woman will "get nearer to God by abiding by its precepts, than by any other book."

This is my prayer, that the Book of Mormon may become the keystone of our lives.

Chapter 4

The Gift
of Modern Revelation

I wish to give thanks to our Father in Heaven for the gift of modern revelation and particularly for the books of latter-day scripture which He has given us.

I love the Bible, both the Old and the New Testaments. It is a source of great truth. It teaches us about the life and ministry of the Master. From its pages we learn of the hand of God in directing the affairs of His people from the very beginning of the earth's history. It would be difficult to underestimate the impact the Bible has had on the history of the world. Its pages have blessed the lives of generations.

But as generation followed generation, no additional scripture came forth to the children of men. Without additional revelation to guide them, men began to interpret the Bible differently. Numerous churches and creeds developed, each using the Bible as its authoritative source.

But this in no way lessens the worth of the Bible. That sacred and holy book has been of inestimable worth to the children of men. In fact, it was a passage from the Bible that inspired the Prophet Joseph Smith to go to a grove of trees near his home and kneel in prayer. What followed was the glorious vision that commenced the restoration of the fulness of the gospel of Jesus Christ to the earth. That vision also began the process of bringing forth new scripture to stand shoulder to shoulder with the Bible in bearing witness to a wicked world that Jesus is the Christ and that God lives and loves His children and is still intimately involved in their salvation and exaltation.

Through the prophet Nephi, the Lord warned against those who might say that the Bible was all the scripture the world would need. He said:

"Know ye not that there are more nations than one? Know ye not that I, the Lord your God, have created all men, . . . and I bring forth my word unto the children of men, yea, even upon all the nations of the earth? . . .

"Know ye not that the testimony of two nations is a witness unto you that I am God, that I remember one nation like unto another? . . .

"And I do this that I may prove unto many that I am the same yesterday, today, and forever." (2 Nephi 29:7–9.)

Today, we have three new books of scripture: the Book of Mormon, the Doctrine and Covenants, and the Pearl of Great Price. I love all of these sacred volumes. I would like to refer particularly to the Book of Mormon and the Doctrine and Covenants. Each of these two books of modern scripture contains a powerful proclamation to the world. The Book of Mormon title page declares its purpose is threefold: to show what great things the Lord has done, to teach of the covenants of the Lord, and to convince both Jew and Gentile that Jesus is the Christ.

Section 1 of the Doctrine and Covenants is the Lord's preface to the book. The Doctrine and Covenants is the only book in the world that has a preface written by the Lord Himself. In that preface He declares to the world that His voice is unto all men (see D&C 1:2), that the coming of the Lord is nigh (D&C 1:12), and that the truths found in the Doctrine and Covenants will all be fulfilled (see D&C 1:37–38).

Each of these two great latter-day scriptures bears powerful and eloquent witness of the Lord Jesus Christ. Virtually every page of both the Doctrine and Covenants and the Book of Mormon teaches about the Master — His great love for His children and His atoning sacrifice — and teaches us how to live so that we can return to Him and our Heavenly Father.

Each of these two great latter-day books of scripture contains the knowledge and the power to help us live better lives in a time of great wickedness and evil. Those who carefully and prayerfully search the pages of these books will find comfort, counsel, guidance, and the quiet power to improve their lives.

Of the Book of Mormon, President Marion G. Romney has said:

"If our young folks are traditioned in the teachings of the Book of Mormon, they will not only be inspired with righteous courage to choose the right, ... they will also be so schooled in the principles of the gospel of Jesus Christ that they will know what is right.

"From almost every page of the book, there will come to them a moving testimony that Jesus is indeed the Christ, the Son of the Living God, our Redeemer and Savior. *This witness alone will be a sustaining anchor in every storm.*" (See *Conference Report,* April 1960, p. 112; italics added.)

Speaking of the revelations in the Doctrine and Covenants, President Joseph Fielding Smith said that "if we will put them into practice, if we will keep the commandments of the Lord, we will know the truth and there shall be no weapon formed against us that shall prosper. There shall be no false doctrines, no teaching of men that will deceive us. . . . [I]f we will search these revelations then we will be fortified against errors and we will be made strong." (See *Conference Report,* October 1931, p. 17.)

Many years before the coming of the Savior to this earth, the prophet Enoch saw the latter days. He observed the great wickedness that would prevail on the earth at this time and foretold the "great tribulations" that would result from such wickedness; but in the midst of what was otherwise a very gloomy prophecy, the Lord promised, "But my people will I preserve." (Moses 7:61.) How would He do so? Note what the Lord Himself promised He would do to preserve His people. He said:

"And *righteousness will I send down out of heaven;* and *truth will I send forth out of the earth,* to bear testimony of mine Only Begotten; . . . and *righteousness and truth* will I cause to sweep the earth as with a flood, to gather out mine elect from the four quarters of the earth, unto a place which I shall prepare." (Moses 7:62; italics added.)

The Lord promised, therefore, that righteousness would come from heaven and truth out of the earth. We have seen the marvelous fulfillment of that prophecy in our generation. The Book of Mormon has come forth out of the earth, filled with truth, serving as the very "keystone of our religion." God has also sent down righteousness from heaven. The Father Himself appeared with His Son to the Prophet Joseph Smith. The angel Moroni, John the Baptist, Peter, James, and numerous other angels were directed by heaven to restore the necessary powers to the kingdom. Further, the Prophet Joseph Smith received revelation after revelation from the heavens during those first critical years of the Church's growth. These revelations have been preserved for us in the Doctrine and Covenants.

These two great works of scripture, then, become a major tool in the Lord's hand for preserving His people in the latter days. The Book of Mormon, written under the hand of inspiration for our day, preserved through the centuries to come forth in our time, translated by the gift and power of God, is the keystone of our religion. It is the keystone of our doctrine. It is the keystone of our testimony. It is a keystone in the witness of Jesus Christ. It is a keystone in helping us avoid the deceptions of the evil one in these latter days. Satan rages in the hearts of men and has power over all of his dominions. (See D&C 1:35.) But the Book of Mormon has greater power — power to reveal false doctrine, power to help us overcome temptations, power to help us get closer to God than any other book.

The Book of Mormon must be reenthroned in the minds and hearts of our people. We must honor it by reading it, by studying it, by taking its precepts into our lives and transforming them into lives required of the true followers of Christ. Speaking of the central role of the Book of Mormon in our worship, President Joseph Fielding Smith said: "It seems to me that any member of this Church would never be satisfied until he or she had read the Book of Mormon time and time again, and thoroughly considered it so that he or she could bear witness that it is in very deed a record with the inspiration of the Almighty upon it, and that its history is true. . . .

"No member of this Church can stand approved in the presence of God who has not seriously and carefully

read the Book of Mormon." (Conference Report, October 1961, p. 18; italics added.)

Likewise, the Doctrine and Covenants becomes an essential part of our spiritual life. The Prophet Joseph Smith said, "In these infant days of the Church, there was great anxiety to obtain the word of the Lord upon every subject that in any way concerned our salvation." (*History of the Church* 1:207.)

Thus, the Doctrine and Covenants is a glorious book of scripture given directly to our generation. It contains the will of the Lord for us in these last days that precede the second coming of Christ. It contains many truths and doctrines not fully revealed in other scripture. Like the Book of Mormon, it will strengthen those who carefully and prayerfully study from its pages.

Do we, as Saints of the Most High God, treasure the word He has preserved for us at so great a cost? Are we using these books of latter-day revelation to bless our lives and resist the powers of the evil one? This is the purpose for which they were given. How can we not stand condemned before the Lord if we treat them lightly by letting them do no more than gather dust on our shelves?

I bear my solemn witness that these books contain the mind and the will of the Lord for us in these days of trial and tribulation. They stand with the Bible to give witness of the Lord and his work. These books contain the voice of the Lord to us in these latter days. May we turn to them with full purpose of heart and use them in the way the Lord wishes them to be used.

Chapter 5

The Book of Mormon
and the
Doctrine and Covenants

The Book of Mormon and the Doctrine and Covenants are bound together as revelations from Israel's God to gather and prepare His people for the second coming of the Lord.

The bringing forth of these sacred volumes of scripture "for the salvation of a ruined world" cost "the best blood of the nineteenth century"—that of Joseph Smith and his brother Hyrum. (D&C 135:6.)

Each divine witness contains a great proclamation to all the world—the title page of the Book of Mormon, and section 1, the Lord's preface to the Doctrine and Covenants. The Book of Mormon and the Doctrine and Covenants testify of each other. You cannot believe one and not the other.

"This generation," said the Lord to Joseph Smith, "shall have my word through you." (D&C 5:10.) And so it has through the Book of Mormon, the Doctrine and Covenants, and other modern revelations.

The Book of Mormon testifies of modern books of scripture. It refers to them as "other books" and "last records" which "establish the truth" of the Bible and make known the "plain and precious things which have been taken away" from the Bible. (1 Nephi 13:39–40.)

Excluding the witnesses to the Book of Mormon, the Doctrine and Covenants is by far the greatest external witness and evidence which we have from the Lord that the Book of Mormon is true. At least thirteen sections in the Doctrine and Covenants give us confirming knowledge and divine witness that the Book of Mormon is the word of God. (See D&C 1; 3; 5; 8; 10–11; 17–18; 20; 27; 42; 84; 135.)

The Doctrine and Covenants is the binding link between the Book of Mormon and the continuing work of the Restoration through the Prophet Joseph Smith and his successors.

In the Doctrine and Covenants we learn of temple work, eternal families, the degrees of glory, Church organization, and many other great truths of the Restoration.

"Search these commandments," said the Lord of the Doctrine and Covenants, "for they are true and faithful, and the prophecies and promises which are in them shall all be fulfilled.

"What I the Lord have spoken, I have spoken, and I excuse not myself; and though the heavens and the earth pass away, my word shall not pass away, but shall all be fulfilled, whether by mine own voice or by the voice of my servants, it is the same." (D&C 1:37–38.)

The Book of Mormon brings men to Christ. The Doctrine and Covenants brings men to Christ's kingdom, even The Church of Jesus Christ of Latter-day Saints, "the only true and living church upon the face of the whole earth." (D&C 1:30.) I know that.

The Book of Mormon is the keystone of our religion, and the Doctrine and Covenants is the capstone, with continuing latter-day revelation. The Lord has placed His stamp of approval on both the keystone and the capstone.

The ancient preparation of the Book of Mormon, its preservation, and its publication verify Nephi's words that "the Lord knoweth all things from the beginning; wherefore, he prepareth a way to accomplish all his works among the children of men; for behold, he hath all power unto the fulfilling of all his words." (1 Nephi 9:6.)

We are not required to prove that the Book of Mormon is true or is an authentic record through external evidences—though there are many. It never has been the case, nor is it so now, that the studies of the learned will prove the Book of Mormon true or false. The origin, preparation, translation, and verification of the truth of the Book of Mormon have all been retained in the hands of the Lord, and the Lord makes no mistakes. You can be assured of that.

God has built in his own proof system of the Book of Mormon as found in Moroni, chapter 10, and in the testimonies of the Three and the Eight Witnesses and in various sections of the Doctrine and Covenants.

We each need to get our own testimony of the Book of Mormon through the Holy Ghost. Then our testimony, coupled with the Book of Mormon, should be shared with others so that they, too, can know through the Holy Ghost of its truthfulness.

Nephi testifies that the Book of Mormon contains the "words of Christ" and that if people "believe in Christ," they will believe in the Book of Mormon. (2 Nephi 33:10.)

It is important that in our teaching we make use of the language of holy writ. Alma said, "I . . . do command you in the language of him who hath commanded me." (Alma 5:61.)

The words and the way they are used in the Book of

Mormon by the Lord should become our source of understanding and should be used by us in teaching gospel principles.

God uses the power of the word of the Book of Mormon as an instrument to change people's lives: "As the preaching of the word had a great tendency to lead the people to do that which was just—yea, it had had more powerful effect upon the minds of the people than the sword, or anything else, which had happened unto them—therefore Alma thought it was expedient that they should try the virtue of the word of God." (Alma 31:5.)

Alma reminded his brethren of the Church how God delivered their fathers' souls from hell: "Behold, they were in the midst of darkness; nevertheless, their souls were illuminated by the light of the everlasting word." (Alma 5:7.)

We need to use the everlasting word to awaken those in deep sleep so they will awake "unto God."

I am deeply concerned about what we are doing to teach the Saints at all levels the gospel of Jesus Christ as completely and authoritatively as do the Book of Mormon and the Doctrine and Covenants. By this I mean teaching the "great plan of the Eternal God," to use the words of Amulek. (Alma 34:9.)

Are we using the messages and the method of teaching found in the Book of Mormon and other scriptures of the Restoration to teach this great plan of the Eternal God?

There are many examples of teaching this great plan, but I will quote just one. It is Mormon's summary statement of Aaron's work as a missionary:

"And it came to pass that when Aaron saw that the king would believe his words, he began from the creation of Adam, reading the scriptures unto the king—how God created man after his own image, and that God gave him commandments, and that because of transgression, man had fallen.

"And Aaron did expound unto him the scriptures from the creation of Adam, laying the fall of man before him, and their carnal state and also the plan of redemption, which was prepared from the foundation of the world, through Christ, for all whosoever would believe on his name.

"And since man had fallen he could not merit anything of himself; but the sufferings and death of Christ atone for their sins, through faith and repentance." (Alma 22:12–14.)

The Book of Mormon Saints knew that the plan of redemption must start with the account of the fall of Adam. In the words of Moroni, "By Adam came the fall of man. And because of the fall of man came Jesus Christ, . . . and because of Jesus Christ came the redemption of man." (Mormon 9:12.)

Just as a man does not really desire food until he is hungry, so he does not desire the salvation of Christ until he knows why he needs Christ.

No one adequately and properly knows why he needs Christ until he understands and accepts the doctrine of the Fall and its effect upon all mankind. And no other book in the world explains this vital doctrine nearly as well as the Book of Mormon.

We all need to take a careful inventory of our performance and also the performance of those over whom we preside to be sure that we are teaching the "great plan of the Eternal God" to the Saints.

Are we accepting and teaching what the revelations tell us about the Creation, Adam and the fall of man, and redemption from that fall through the atonement of Christ? Do we frequently review the crucial questions which Alma asks the members of the Church in the fifth chapter of Alma in the Book of Mormon?

Do we understand and are we effective in teaching and preaching the Atonement? What personal meaning does the Lord's suffering in Gethsemane and on Calvary have for each of us?

What does redemption from the Fall mean to us? In the words of Alma, do we "sing the song of redeeming love"? (Alma 5:26.)

Now, what should be the source for teaching the great plan of the Eternal God? The scriptures, of course—particularly the Book of Mormon. This should also include the other modern-day revelations. These should be coupled with the words of the apostles and prophets and the promptings of the Spirit.

Alma "commanded them that they should teach nothing save it were the things which he had taught, and which had been spoken by the mouth of the holy prophets." (Mosiah 18:19.)

The Doctrine and Covenants states, "Let them journey from thence preaching the word by the way, saying none other things than that which the prophets and apostles have written, and that which is taught them by the Comforter through the prayer of faith." (D&C 52:9.)

Now, after we teach the great plan of the Eternal God, we must personally bear our testimonies of its truthfulness.

Alma, after giving a great message to the Saints about being born again and the need for them to experience a "mighty change" in their hearts, sealed his teaching with his testimony in these words:

"And this is not all. Do ye not suppose that I know of these things myself? Behold, I testify unto you that I do know that these things whereof I have spoken are true. And how do ye suppose that I know of their surety?

"Behold, I say unto you they are made known unto me by the Holy Spirit of God. Behold, I have fasted and prayed many days that I might know these things of myself. And now I do know of myself that they are true; for the Lord God hath made them manifest unto me by his Holy Spirit; and this is the spirit of revelation which is in me." (Alma 5:45–46.)

Later Amulek joined Alma as his missionary companion. After Alma had delivered to the Zoramites his message concerning faith in Christ, Amulek sealed with his testimony the message of his companion in these words:

"And now, behold, I will testify unto you of myself that these things are true. Behold, I say unto you, that I do know that Christ shall come among the children of men, to take upon him the transgressions of his people, and that he shall atone for the sins of the world; for the Lord God hath spoken it." (Alma 34:8.)

In His preface to the Doctrine and Covenants, the Lord said that the "voice of warning shall be unto all people, by the mouths of my disciples, whom I have chosen in these last days." (D&C 1:4.)

The responsibility of the seed of Abraham, which we are, is to be missionaries to "bear this ministry and Priesthood unto all nations." (Abraham 2:9.) Moses bestowed upon Joseph Smith in the Kirtland Temple the keys to gather Israel. (See D&C 110:11.)

Now, what is the instrument that God has designed for this gathering? It is the same instrument that is designed to convince the world that Jesus is the Christ, that Joseph Smith is His prophet, and that The Church of Jesus Christ of Latter-day Saints is true. It is that scripture which is the keystone of our religion.

It is that most correct book which, if men will abide by its precepts, will get them closer to God than any other book. It is the Book of Mormon.

God bless us all to use all the scriptures, but in particular the instrument He designed to bring us to Christ—the Book of Mormon, the keystone of our religion—along with its companion volume, the capstone, the Doctrine and Covenants, the instrument to bring us to Christ's kingdom, The Church of Jesus Christ of Latter-day Saints.

Now, by virtue of the sacred priesthood in me vested, I invoke the blessings of the Lord upon the Latter-day Saints and upon good people everywhere.

I bless you with added power to endure in righteousness amidst the growing onslaught of wickedness.

I promise you that as you more diligently study modern revelation on gospel subjects, your power to teach and preach will be magnified and you will so move the cause of Zion that added numbers will enter into the house of the Lord as well as the mission field.

I bless you with increased desire to flood the earth with the Book of Mormon, to gather out from the world the elect of God who are yearning for the truth but know not where to find it.

I promise you that, with increased attendance in the temples of our God, you shall receive increased personal revelation to bless your life as you bless those who have died.

I testify that the Book of Mormon is the word of God. Jesus is the Christ. Joseph Smith is His prophet. The Church of Jesus Christ of Latter-day Saints is true.

Chapter 6

The Savior's Visit to America

I have been deeply touched by the response of members of the Church who have heeded counsel to read and reread the word of the Lord as set forth in the Book of Mormon. This has resulted in increased spirituality and is helping to cleanse the inner vessel.

Adults, youth, and children have borne powerful testimonies as to how the Book of Mormon has changed their lives. My life, too, continues to be changed by this sacred volume of scripture.

I have been reading again the marvelous account in the Book of Mormon of the visit of the resurrected Savior to the American continent. I have been deeply impressed with the beauty and power of this scriptural account in 3 Nephi, and with its great value for our time and our generation.

The record of the Nephite history just prior to the Savior's visit reveals many parallels to our own day as we anticipate the Savior's second coming. The Nephite civilization had reached great heights. They were prosperous and industrious. They had built many cities with great highways connecting them. They engaged in shipping and trade. They built temples and palaces.

But, as so often happens, the people rejected the Lord. Pride became commonplace. Dishonesty and immorality were widespread. Secret combinations flourished because, as Helaman tells us, the Gadianton robbers "had seduced the more part of the righteous until they had come down to believe in their works and partake of their spoils." (Helaman 6:38.) "The people began to be distinguished by ranks, according to their riches and their chances for learning." (3 Nephi 6:12.) And "Satan had great power, unto the stirring up of the people to do all manner of iniquity, and to the puffing them up with pride, tempting them to seek for power, and authority, and riches, and the vain things of the world," even as today. (3 Nephi 6:15.)

Mormon noted that the Nephites "did not sin ignorantly, for they knew the will of God concerning them." (3 Nephi 6:18.)

There were but few righteous among them. (3 Nephi 6:14.) Nephi led the Church with great power and performed many miracles, yet "there were but few who were converted unto the Lord." (3 Nephi 7:21.) The people as a whole rejected the Lord. They stoned the prophets and persecuted those who sought to follow Christ.

And then the God of nature intervened, even Jesus Christ. A storm began such as had never before been known in all the land. Lightning flashed and thunder shook the earth. Violent winds carried people away, never to be seen again.

"Many great and notable cities were sunk, and many were burned, and many were shaken till the buildings thereof had fallen to the earth, and the inhabitants thereof were slain." (3 Nephi 8:14.) "The whole face of the land was changed." (3 Nephi 8:12.)

For three hours the forces of nature raged. Finally when the thunder, lightning, storm, tempest, and quaking had ceased, a thick darkness settled over the land. For three days no light could be seen, no candle could be lit. The vapor of darkness was so thick that it could be felt, "and there was great mourning and howling and weeping among all the people."

They were heard to cry and mourn, saying: "O that we had repented before this great and terrible day, and had not killed and stoned the prophets, and cast them out." (3 Nephi 8:23–25.)

Then a voice began to speak — a voice from the heavens that was heard throughout the entire land.

The voice spoke of the terrible destruction and announced that this was a direct result of the wickedness and the abominations among the people.

Imagine the feelings of the people when the voice asked, "Will ye not now return unto me, and repent of your sins, and be converted, that I may heal you?" (3 Nephi 9:13.)

Then the voice identified itself: "Behold, I am Jesus Christ the Son of God." (3 Nephi 9:15.) It was the voice of the very person who had been mocked and ridiculed and rejected by the wicked. It was the voice of Him whom the prophets proclaimed and for whom they were stoned and killed. It was the voice of the Master!

He declared that by Him redemption came, that in Him the law of Moses was fulfilled, and that they were to offer a sacrifice unto Him of a broken heart and a contrite spirit.

When the darkness had dispersed, a great multitude gathered around the temple in the land of Bountiful.

39

Twenty-five hundred men, women, and children had come together. As they were conversing about this Jesus Christ, of whom the sign had been given concerning his death, they once again heard the voice.

Mormon tells us that "it was not a harsh voice, neither was it a loud voice; nevertheless, and notwithstanding it being a small voice it did pierce them that did hear to the center, insomuch that there was no part of their frame that it did not cause to quake; yea, it did pierce them to the very soul, and did cause their hearts to burn." (3 Nephi 11:3.) The first time and the second time the voice spoke, the people heard it but could not understand it.

The record then states that "again the third time they did hear the voice, and did open their ears to hear it. . . .

"And behold, the third time they did understand the voice which they heard; and it said unto them:

"Behold my Beloved Son, in whom I am well pleased, in whom I have glorified my name—hear ye him." (3 Nephi 11:5–7.)

How few people in all the history of the world have heard the actual voice of God the Father speaking to them. As the people looked heavenward, "they saw a Man descending out of heaven; and he was clothed in a white robe; and he came down and stood in the midst of them." (3 Nephi 11:8.)

A glorious, resurrected being, a member of the Godhead, the Creator of innumerable worlds, the God of Abraham, Isaac, and Jacob, stood before their very eyes!

"And it came to pass that he stretched forth his hand and spake unto the people, saying:

"Behold, I am Jesus Christ, whom the prophets testified shall come into the world.

"And behold, I am the light and the life of the world; and I have drunk out of that bitter cup which the Father hath given me, and have glorified the Father in taking upon me the sins of the world, in the which I have suffered the will of the Father in all things from the beginning." (3 Nephi 11:9–11.)

The whole multitude fell to the earth. Jesus commanded them to rise and come forth unto Him. He invited them to thrust their hands into His side and feel the prints of the nails in His hands and feet. One by one each of the twenty-five hundred present went forth.

Indeed they "did see with their eyes and did feel with their hands, and did know of a surety and did bear record, that it was he, of whom it was written by the prophets, that should come." (3 Nephi 11:15.)

When the last one had stood face to face with the Savior and had come to know with an absolute surety of the reality of His resurrection, "they did cry out with one accord, saying: "Hosanna! Blessed be the name of the Most High God! And they did fall down at the feet of Jesus, and did worship him." (3 Nephi 11:16–17.)

He called the faithful prophet Nephi and others and commissioned them with power and authority to baptize in His name.

The Savior taught the people: "Ye must repent, and be baptized in my name, and become as a little child, or ye can in nowise inherit the kingdom of God." (3 Nephi 11:38.)

He gave them the glorious sermon which we today call the Sermon on the Mount.

And then He said: "I perceive that ye are weak, that ye cannot understand all my words which I am commanded of the Father to speak unto you at this time.

"Therefore, go ye unto your homes, and ponder upon the things which I have said, and ask of the Father, in my name, that ye may understand, and prepare your minds for the morrow, and I come unto you again." (3 Nephi 17:2–3.)

As the Master announced His departure, "He cast his eyes round about again on the multitude, and beheld they were in tears, and did look steadfastly upon him as if they would ask him to tarry a little longer with them." (3 Nephi 17:5.)

Moved with tender compassion, the resurrected Lord commanded them to bring their sick, their handicapped, their diseased.

"And it came to pass that when he had thus spoken, all the multitude, with one accord, did go forth with their sick and their afflicted, and their lame, and with their blind, and with their dumb, and with all them that were afflicted in any manner; and he did heal them every one as they were brought forth unto him." (3 Nephi 17:9.)

The Savior then called for the little children. He commanded the multitude to kneel as He prayed to the Father.

Mormon tells us that "no tongue can speak, neither can there be written by any man, neither can the hearts of men conceive so great and marvelous things" as were spoken in that prayer. (3 Nephi 17:17.) Then, weeping with joy, Jesus took the little children to Him one by one and blessed them. Finally, turning to the multitude, He said, "Behold your little ones." (3 Nephi 17:23.)

As they lifted their eyes, "they saw the heavens open, and they saw angels descending out of heaven as it were in the midst of fire; and they came down and encircled those little ones about, and they were encircled about with fire; and the angels did minister unto them." (3 Nephi 17:24.)

Remarkable events occurred on that glorious day and the days that followed. It is clear that 3 Nephi contains some of the most moving and powerful passages in all scripture. It testifies of Jesus Christ, His prophets, and the doctrines of salvation. What a blessing it would be if every family would frequently read together 3 Nephi, discuss its sacred contents, and then determine how they can liken it unto themselves and apply its teachings in their lives!

Third Nephi is a book that should be read and read again. Its testimony of the resurrected Christ in America is given in purity and beauty. As the Savior prepared to leave His disciples, He said unto them:

"Behold I have given unto you my gospel, and this is the gospel which I have given unto you—that I came into the world to do the will of my Father, because my Father sent me.

"And my Father sent me that I might be lifted up upon the cross; and after that I had been lifted up upon the cross, that I might draw all men unto me, that as I have been lifted up by men even so should men be lifted up by the Father, to stand before me, to be judged of their works, whether they be good or whether they be evil. . . .

"And it shall come to pass, that whoso repenteth and is baptized in my name shall be filled; and if he endureth to the end, behold, him will I hold guiltless before my Father at that day when I shall stand to judge the world. . . .

"And no unclean thing can enter into his kingdom; therefore nothing entereth into his rest save it be those who have washed their garments in my blood, because of their faith, and the repentance of all their sins, and their faithfulness unto the end.

"Now this is the commandment: Repent, all ye ends of the earth, and come unto me and be baptized in my name, that ye may be sanctified by the reception of the Holy Ghost, that ye may stand spotless before me at the last day.

"Verily, verily, I say unto you, this is my gospel." (3 Nephi 27:13–14, 16, 19–21.)

The mission of the resurrected Christ did not end with His appearance to those in the Holy Land or even to those in ancient America, for the continuing miracle is that He has revealed Himself again to men in our day.

In section 76 of the Doctrine and Covenants the Prophet Joseph Smith records the marvelous vision which he and Sidney Rigdon had. The Prophet declared:

"And now, after the many testimonies which have been given of him, this is the testimony, last of all, which we give of him: That he lives!

"For we saw him, even on the right hand of God; and we heard the voice bearing record that he is the Only Begotten of the Father—

"That by him, and through him, and of him, the worlds are and were created, and the inhabitants thereof are begotten sons and daughters unto God." (D&C 76:22–24.)

Now what does all of this mean to us? It means that as Christ lives today with a resurrected body, so shall we. It means that life is a probation, to be followed by death, resurrection, and judgment.

In the Book of Mormon, the keystone of our religion, we read: "Death comes upon mankind, . . . nevertheless there was a space granted unto man in which he might repent; therefore this life became a probationary state; a time to prepare to meet God; a time to prepare for that endless state which has been spoken of by us, which is after the resurrection of the dead." (Alma 12:24.)

All shall rise from the dead. The spirit and the body shall be reunited again in its perfect form; both limb and joint shall be restored to its proper frame, and we shall be brought to stand before God, and be arraigned before the bar of Christ the Son, and God the Father, and the Holy Spirit, to be judged according to our works, whether they be good or whether they be evil. (See Alma 11:42–44.)

In light of our mortal probation, our future resurrection, and our final judgment, we need to remember the question which the resurrected Lord posed to His disciples as recorded in 3 Nephi in the Book of Mormon.

He asked them, "Therefore, what manner of men ought ye to be?" And He answered, "Verily I say unto you, even as I am." (3 Nephi 27:27.)

He is our Exemplar, our Redeemer, our Lord.

I testify that 3 Nephi is a true account of the resurrected Christ's visit to ancient America and contains His teachings in their pristine truth. I testify that Jesus is the Christ and that He stands at the head of His Church today, even The Church of Jesus Christ of Latter-day Saints. I testify that He will come again in power and great glory and that He will leave nothing undone for our eternal welfare.

May we daily be the manner of men He is and thus be prepared to meet and dwell with Him.

Chapter 7

Joy in Christ

Without Christ there can be no fulness of joy. In our premortal state, we shouted for joy as the plan of salvation was unfolded to our view. (See Job 38:7.)

It was there our elder brother Jesus, the firstborn in the spirit of our Father's children, volunteered to redeem us from our sins. He became our foreordained Savior, the Lamb "slain from the foundation of the world." (Moses 7:47.)

Thanks be to God the Son for the offering of Himself. And thanks be to God the Father that He sent Him. "For God so loved the world, that he gave his only begotten Son." (John 3:16.)

Jesus was a God in the pre-earthly existence. Our Father in Heaven gave Him a name above all others — the Christ. We have a volume of scripture whose major mission is to convince the world that Jesus is the Christ. It is the Book of Mormon. It is another testament of Jesus Christ and "the most correct of any book on earth."

In its pages we read that "there shall be no other name given nor any other way nor means whereby salvation can come unto the children of men, only in and through the name of Christ, the Lord Omnipotent." (Mosiah 3:17.)

As far as man is concerned, we must build "upon the rock of our Redeemer, who is Christ." (Helaman 5:12.)

The first and great commandment is to love Him and His Father. (See Matthew 22:37–38.)

Jesus Christ is "the Father of heaven and earth, the Creator of all things from the beginning." (Mosiah 3:8.)

"Wherefore," declared Jacob in the Book of Mormon, "if God being able to speak and the world was, and to speak and man was created, O then, why not able to command the earth, or the workmanship of his hands upon the face of it, according to his will and pleasure?" (Jacob 4:9.) God, the Creator, commands His creations even at this very moment.

Every prophet from the days of Adam knew of and testified of the divine ministry of the mortal Messiah. Moses prophesied concerning the coming of the Messiah. (See Mosiah 13:33–35.)

"We knew of Christ, and we had a hope of his glory many hundred years before his coming," reported Jacob in the Book of Mormon. (Jacob 4:4.)

In that same volume of scripture is recorded the manifestation of the Christ in His spirit body to the brother of Jared. "This body, which ye now behold," said the Lord, "is the body of my spirit; and man have I created after the body of my spirit; and even as I appear unto thee to be in the spirit will I appear unto my people in the flesh." (Ether 3:16.) And so He did.

He was the Only Begotten Son of our Heavenly Father in the flesh—the only child whose mortal body was begotten by our Heavenly Father. His mortal mother, Mary, was called a virgin, both before and after she gave birth. (See 1 Nephi 11:20.)

And so the premortal God; the God of the whole earth; the Jehovah of the Old Testament; the God of Abraham,

Isaac, and Jacob; the Lawgiver; the God of Israel; the promised Messiah was born a babe in Bethlehem.

King Benjamin prophesied of Christ's advent and ministry in this manner:

"For behold, the time cometh, and is not far distant, that with power, the Lord Omnipotent who reigneth, who was, and is from all eternity to all eternity, shall come down from heaven among the children of men, and shall dwell in a tabernacle of clay, and shall go forth amongst men, working mighty miracles, such as healing the sick, raising the dead, causing the lame to walk, the blind to receive their sight, and the deaf to hear, and curing all manner of diseases.

"And he shall cast out devils, or the evil spirits which dwell in the hearts of the children of men.

"And lo, he shall suffer temptations, and pain of body, hunger, thirst, and fatigue, even more than man can suffer, except it be unto death; for behold, blood cometh from every pore, so great shall be his anguish for the wickedness and the abominations of his people.

"And he shall be called Jesus Christ, the Son of God, the Father of heaven and earth, the Creator of all things from the beginning; and his mother shall be called Mary." (Mosiah 3:5–8.)

The Lord testified, "I came into the world to do the will of my Father, because my Father sent me. And my Father sent me that I might be lifted up upon the cross." (3 Nephi 27:13–14.) And so He was.

In Gethsemane and on Calvary, He worked out the infinite and eternal Atonement. It was the greatest single act of love in recorded history. Then followed His death and resurrection.

Thus He became our Redeemer—redeeming all of us from physical death, and redeeming those of us from spiritual death who will obey the laws and ordinances of the gospel.

His resurrection is well attested in the Bible. The Book of Mormon records the resurrected Lord's appearance on the American continent.

Today in Christ's restored church, The Church of Jesus Christ of Latter-day Saints, He is revealing Himself and His will—from the first prophet of the Restoration, even Joseph Smith, to the present.

And now, what must we do? Why, we must do the same as the Wise Men of old. They sought out the Christ and found Him. And so must we. Those who are wise still seek Him today.

"I would commend you," urged Moroni, "to seek this Jesus of whom the prophets and apostles have written." (Ether 12:41.) And God has provided the means—the holy scriptures, particularly the Book of Mormon—that all who seek may know that Jesus is the Christ.

In his *Lectures on Faith*, the Prophet Joseph Smith listed six divine attributes of God that men must understand in order to have faith in Him. (See *Lectures on Faith*, 3:41.) The Book of Mormon bears constant witness that Christ possesses all these attributes.

First, God is the Creator and upholder of all things. King Benjamin said, "He created all things, . . . he has all wisdom, and all power." (Mosiah 4:9.)

Second, God is distinguished by the excellency of His character, His mercy, long-suffering, and goodness. Alma testified that Christ is "full of grace, equity, and truth, full of patience, mercy, and long-suffering." (Alma 9:26.)

Third, God changes not. Mormon revealed that "God is not . . . a changeable being; but he is unchangeable from all eternity to all eternity." (Moroni 8:18.)

Fourth, God cannot lie. The brother of Jared declared, "Thou art a God of truth, and canst not lie." (Ether 3:12.)

Fifth, God is no respecter of persons. Mormon testified that "God is not a partial God." (Moroni 8:18.)

Sixth, God is a God of love. Of this divine attribute Nephi wrote that the Lord "doeth not anything save it be for the benefit of the world; for he loveth the world, even that he layeth down his own life." (2 Nephi 26:24.)

The Book of Mormon was designed by Deity to bring men to Christ and to His church. Both we and our non-member friends may know that the Book of Mormon is true by putting it to the divine test which Moroni proposed. (See Moroni 10:3–5.)

What a gift it would be to receive a greater knowledge of the Lord! What a gift it would be to share that knowledge with others!

To that end may I encourage you not only to read the biblical account of Christ's resurrection, but to read and share with a nonmember acquaintance the Book of Mormon account of Christ's personal manifestation to those in America following his resurrection.

Give them or lend them a copy of the Book of Mormon, even your own copy if necessary. It could bless them eternally.

In conclusion, in Book of Mormon language, we need to "believe in Christ and deny him not." (2 Nephi 25:28.) We need to trust in Christ and not in the arm of flesh. (See 2 Nephi 4:34.) We need to "come unto Christ, and be perfected in him." (Moroni 10:32.) We need to come "with a broken heart and a contrite spirit" (3 Nephi 12:19), hungering and thirsting after righteousness (see 3 Nephi 12:6). We need to come "feasting upon the word of Christ" (2 Nephi 31:20), as we receive it through His scriptures, His anointed, and His Holy Spirit.

In short, we need to follow "the example of the Son of the living God" (2 Nephi 31:16) and be the "manner of men" He is (see 3 Nephi 27:27).

With Moroni, I testify that "the eternal purposes of the Lord shall roll on, until all his promises shall be fulfilled." (Mormon 8:22.)

Not many years hence Christ will come again. He will come in power and might as King of Kings and Lord of Lords. And ultimately every knee shall bow and every tongue confess that Jesus is the Christ.

But I testify *now* that Jesus is the Christ, that Joseph Smith is His prophet, that the Book of Mormon is the word of God, and that His church, The Church of Jesus Christ of Latter-day Saints, is true, and that Christ is at its helm.

Chapter 8

Come Unto Christ

The major mission of the Book of Mormon, as recorded on its title page, is "to the convincing of the Jew and Gentile that Jesus is the Christ, the eternal God, manifesting himself unto all nations."

The honest seeker after truth can gain the testimony that Jesus is the Christ as he prayerfully ponders the inspired words of the Book of Mormon.

Over one-half of all the verses in the Book of Mormon refer to our Lord. Some form of Christ's name is mentioned more frequently per verse in the Book of Mormon than even in the New Testament.

He is given over one hundred different names in the Book of Mormon. Those names have a particular significance in describing His divine nature.

Let us consider some of the attributes of our Lord, as found in the Book of Mormon, that show that Jesus is the Christ. Then let us confirm each of those attributes about Him with a brief quote from the Book of Mormon.

He is *Alive:* "The life of the world . . . a life which is endless." (Mosiah 16:9.)

He is *Constant:* "The same yesterday, today, and forever." (2 Nephi 27:23.)

He is the *Creator:* "He created all things, both in heaven and in earth." (Mosiah 4:9.)

He is the *Exemplar:* He "set the example. . . . He said unto the children of men: Follow thou me." (2 Nephi 31:9–10.)

He is *Generous:* "He commandeth none that they shall not partake of his salvation." (2 Nephi 26:24.)

He is *Godly:* He is God. (See 2 Nephi 27:23.)

He is *Good:* "All things which are good cometh of God." (Moroni 7:12.)

He is *Gracious:* "He is full of grace." (2 Nephi 2:6.)

He is the *Healer:* The "sick, and . . . afflicted with all manner of diseases . . . devils and unclean spirits . . . were healed by the power of the Lamb of God." (1 Nephi 11:31.)

He is *Holy:* "O how great the holiness of our God!" (2 Nephi 9:20.)

He is *Humble:* "He humbleth himself before the Father." (2 Nephi 31:7.)

He is *Joyful:* "The Father hath given" Him a "fulness of joy." (3 Nephi 28:10.)

He is our *Judge:* We "shall be brought to stand before the bar of God, to be judged of him." (Mosiah 16:10.)

He is *Just:* "The judgments of God are always just." (Mosiah 29:12.)

He is *Kind:* He has "loving kindness . . . towards the children of men." (1 Nephi 19:9.)

He is the *Lawgiver:* He "gave the law." (3 Nephi 15:5.)

He is the *Liberator:* "There is no other head whereby ye can be made free." (Mosiah 5:8.)

He is the *Light:* "The light . . . of the world; yea, a light that is endless, that can never be darkened." (Mosiah 16:9.)

He is *Loving:* "He loveth the world, even that he layeth down his own life." (2 Nephi 26:24.)

He is the *Mediator:* "The great Mediator of all men." (2 Nephi 2:27.)

He is *Merciful:* There is a "multitude of his tender mercies." (1 Nephi 8:8.)

He is *Mighty:* "Mightier than all the earth." (1 Nephi 4:1.)

He is *Miraculous:* A "God of miracles." (2 Nephi 27:23.)

He is *Obedient:* Obedient unto the Father "in keeping his commandments." (2 Nephi 31:7.)

He is *Omnipotent:* He has "all power, both in heaven and in earth." (Mosiah 4:9.)

He is *Omniscient:* "The Lord knoweth all things from the beginning." (1 Nephi 9:6.)

He is our *Redeemer:* "All mankind were in a lost and in a fallen state, and ever would be save they should rely on this Redeemer." (1 Nephi 10:6.)

He is the *Resurrection:* He brought to pass "the resurrection of the dead, being the first that should rise." (2 Nephi 2:8.)

He is *Righteous:* "His ways are righteousness forever." (2 Nephi 1:19.)

He is the *Ruler:* He rules "in the heavens above and in the earth beneath." (2 Nephi 29:7.)

He is our *Savior:* "There is none other name given under heaven save it be this Jesus Christ . . . whereby man can be saved." (2 Nephi 25:20.)

He is *Sinless:* He "suffereth temptation, and yieldeth not to the temptation." (Mosiah 15:5.)

He is *Truthful:* "A God of truth, and canst not lie." (Ether 3:12.)

He is *Wise:* "He has all wisdom." (Mosiah 4:9.)

As I reflect on these and many other marks of our Lord's

divinity, as found in the Book of Mormon, my heart cries out with the hymnist:

> *Oh Lord my God, when I in awesome wonder*
> *Consider all the worlds thy hands have made,*
> *I see the stars, I hear the rolling thunder,*
> *Thy pow'r thruout the universe displayed;*
> *Then sings my soul, my Savior God, to thee,*
> *How great thou art! How great thou art!*
> *("How Great Thou Art," Hymns, 1985, no 86.)*

Once one is convinced, through the Book of Mormon, that Jesus is the Christ, then he must take the next step; he must come unto Christ. Learning the precepts found in what the Prophet Joseph Smith called the most correct book on earth, the Book of Mormon, is but the first step. Abiding by those precepts found in the keystone of our religion gets a man nearer to God than through any other book. Can we not see why we should be reading this book daily and practicing its precepts at all times?

We have an increasing number who have been convinced, through the Book of Mormon, that Jesus is the Christ. Now we need an increasing number who will use the Book of Mormon to become committed to Christ. We need to be convinced and committed.

Let us turn again to the Book of Mormon, this time to learn some principles about coming unto Christ, being committed to Him, centered in Him, and consumed in Him. We will quote but a few of the numerous passages on the matter.

First we need to know that Christ invites us to come unto Him. "Behold, he sendeth an invitation unto all men, for the arms of mercy are extended towards them, . . . yea, he saith: Come unto me and ye shall partake of the fruit of the tree of life." (Alma 5:33–34.)

Come, for He stands "with open arms to receive you." (Mormon 6:17.)

Come, for "he will console you in your afflictions, and he will plead your cause." (Jacob 3:1.)

"Come unto him, and offer your whole souls as an offering unto him." (Omni 1:26.)

As Moroni closed the record of the Jaredite civilization, he wrote, "I would commend you to seek this Jesus of whom the prophets and apostles have written." (Ether 12:41.)

In Moroni's closing words written toward the end of the Nephite civilization, he said, "Yea, come unto Christ, and be perfected in him, . . . and if ye shall deny yourselves of all ungodliness, and love God with all your might, mind and strength, then is his grace sufficient for you." (Moroni 10:32.)

Those who are committed to Christ "stand as witnesses of God at all times and in all things, and in all places" that they may be in "even until death." (Mosiah 18:9.) They "retain the name" of Christ "written always" in their hearts. (Mosiah 5:12.) They take upon themselves "the name of Christ, having a determination to serve him to the end." (Moroni 6:3.)

When we live a Christ-centered life, "we talk of Christ, we rejoice in Christ, we preach of Christ." (2 Nephi 25:26.) We "receive the pleasing word of God, and feast upon his love." (Jacob 3:2.) Even when Nephi's soul was grieved because of his iniquities, he said, "I know in whom I have trusted. My God hath been my support." (2 Nephi 4:19–20.)

We remember Alma's counsel: "Let all thy doings be unto the Lord, and whithersoever thou goest let it be in the Lord; yea, let all thy thoughts be directed unto the Lord; yea, let the affections of thy heart be placed upon

the Lord forever. Counsel with the Lord in all thy doings."
(Alma 37:36–37.)

"Remember, remember," said Helaman, "that it is
upon the rock of our Redeemer, who is Christ, . . . that ye
must build your foundation; that when the devil shall
send forth his mighty winds, . . . [they] shall have no power
over you to drag you down to the gulf of misery." (Helaman 5:12.)

Nephi said, the Lord "hath filled me with his love,
even unto the consuming of my flesh." (2 Nephi 4:21.)
Those who are consumed in Christ "are made alive in
Christ." (2 Nephi 25:25.) They "suffer no manner of afflictions, save it were swallowed up in the joy of Christ."
(Alma 31:38.) They are "clasped in the arms of Jesus."
(Mormon 5:11.) Nephi said, "I glory in my Jesus, for he
hath redeemed my soul." (2 Nephi 33:6.) Lehi said, "I am
encircled about eternally in the arms of his love." (2 Nephi
1:15.)

Let us read the Book of Mormon and be convinced
that Jesus is the Christ. Let us continually reread the Book
of Mormon so that we might more fully come to Christ,
be committed to Him, centered in Him, and consumed
in Him.

We are meeting the adversary every day. The challenges of this era will rival any of the past, and these
challenges will increase both spiritually and temporally.
We must be close to Christ, we must daily take His name
upon us, always remember Him, and keep His commandments.

In the final letter recorded in the Book of Mormon
from Mormon to his son Moroni, he gave counsel that
applies to our day. Both father and son were seeing a
whole Christian civilization fall because its people would
not serve the God of the land, even Jesus Christ. Mormon

wrote, "And now, my beloved son, notwithstanding their hardness, let us labor diligently; for if we should cease to labor, we should be brought under condemnation; for we have a labor to perform whilst in this tabernacle of clay, that we may conquer the enemy of all righteousness, and rest our souls in the kingdom of God." (Moroni 9:6.) You and I have a similar labor to perform now—to conquer the enemy and rest our souls in the kingdom.

Then that great soul Mormon closes his letter to his beloved son, Moroni, with these words.

"My son, be faithful in Christ; and may not the things which I have written grieve thee, to weigh thee down unto death; but may Christ lift thee up, and may his sufferings and death, and the showing his body unto our fathers, and his mercy and long-suffering, and the hope of his glory and of eternal life, rest in your mind forever.

"And may the grace of God the Father, whose throne is high in the heavens, and our Lord Jesus Christ, who sitteth on the right hand of his power, until all things shall become subject unto him, be, and abide with you forever." (Moroni 9:25–26.)

My prayer for each of us is that we too will follow that inspired counsel: "Be faithful in Christ." Then He will lift us up and His grace will be and abide with us forever.

Chapter 9

Born of God

"What think ye of Christ?" (Matthew 22:42.) That question, posed by our Lord, has challenged the world for centuries.

Fortunately for us, God has provided modern scripture, another testament, even the Book of Mormon, for the convincing of the world that Jesus is the Christ. Anyone who will read the Book of Mormon and put it to the divine test that Moroni proposes (see Moroni 10:3–5) can be convinced that Jesus is the Christ. Once that conviction is gained, then comes the question, "Will we choose to follow Him?" The devils believe that Jesus is the Christ, but they choose to follow Lucifer. (See James 2:19; Mark 5:7.)

Throughout the ages prophets have exhorted the people to make up their minds. "Choose you this day whom ye will serve," pled Joshua. (Joshua 24:15.) Elijah thundered, "How long halt ye between two opinions? if the Lord be God, follow him." (1 Kings 18:21.) When you choose to follow Christ, you choose the Way, the Truth, the Life—the right way, the saving truth, the abundant life. (See John 14:6.) "I would commend you to seek this Jesus," states Moroni. (Ether 12:41.)

When you choose to follow Christ, you choose to be

changed. "No man," said President David O. McKay, "can sincerely resolve to apply to his daily life the teachings of Jesus of Nazareth without sensing a change in his own nature. The phrase 'born again' has a deeper significance than many people attach to it. This *changed feeling* may be indescribable, *but it is real.*" (*Conference Report,* April 1962, p. 7.)

Can human hearts be changed? Why, of course! It happens every day in the great missionary work of the Church. It is one of the most widespread of Christ's modern miracles. If it hasn't happened to you—it should.

Our Lord told Nicodemus that "except a man be born again, he cannot see the kingdom of God." (John 3:3.) Of these words President Spencer W. Kimball said, "This is the simple total answer to the weightiest of all questions. . . . To gain eternal life there must be a rebirth, a transformation." (*Conference Report,* April 1958, p. 14.)

President McKay said that Christ called for "an entire revolution" of Nicodemus's "inner man." "His manner of thinking, feeling, and acting with reference to spiritual things would have to undergo a fundamental and permanent change." (*Conference Report,* April 1960, p. 26.)

In addition to the physical ordinance of baptism and the laying on of hands, one must be spiritually born again to gain exaltation and eternal life.

Alma states: "And the Lord said unto me: Marvel not that all mankind, yea, men and women, all nations, kindreds, tongues and people, must be born again; yea, born of God, changed from their carnal and fallen state, to a state of righteousness, being redeemed of God, becoming his sons and daughters;

"And thus they become new creatures; and unless they do this, they can in nowise inherit the kingdom of God." (Mosiah 27:25–26.)

The "change of heart" and "born again" processes are best described in the keystone of our religion, the Book of Mormon.

Those who had been born of God after hearing King Benjamin's address had a mighty change in their hearts. They had "no more disposition to do evil, but to do good continually." (See Mosiah 5:2, 7.)

The fourth chapter of Alma describes a period in Nephite history when "the church began to fail in its progress." (Alma 4:10.) Alma met this challenge by resigning his seat as chief judge in government "and confined himself wholly to the high priesthood" responsibility which was his. (Alma 4:20.)

He bore "down in pure testimony" against the people (see Alma 4:19), and in the fifth chapter of Alma he asks over forty crucial questions. Speaking frankly to the members of the Church, he declared, "I ask of you, my brethren of the church, have ye spiritually been born of God? Have ye received his image in your countenances? Have ye experienced this mighty change in your hearts?" (Alma 5:14.)

He continued, "If ye have experienced a change of heart, and if ye have felt to sing the song of redeeming love, I would ask, can ye feel so now?" (Alma 5:26.)

Would not the progress of the Church increase dramatically today with an increasing number of those who are spiritually reborn? Can you imagine what would happen in our homes? Can you imagine what would happen with an increasing number of copies of the Book of Mormon in the hands of an increasing number of missionaries who know how to use it and who have been born of God? When this happens, we will get the bounteous harvest of souls that the Lord promised. It was the "born of God" Alma who as a missionary was so able to impart the word that many others were also born of God. (See Alma 36:23–26.)

The Lord works from the inside out. The world works from the outside in. The world would take people out of the slums. Christ takes the slums out of people, and then they take themselves out of the slums. The world would mold men by changing their environment. Christ changes men, who then change their environment. The world would shape human behavior, but Christ can change human nature.

"Human nature *can* be changed, here and now," said President McKay, and then he quoted the following:

"You can change human nature. No man who has felt in him the Spirit of Christ even for half a minute can deny this truth. . . .

"You do change human nature, your own human nature, if you surrender it to Christ. Human nature has been changed in the past. Human nature must be changed on an enormous scale in the future, unless the world is to be drowned in its own blood. And only Christ can change it.

"Twelve men did quite a lot to change the world [nineteen hundred] years ago. Twelve simple men." (Quoting Beverly Nichols, in *Stepping Stones to an Abundant Life,* pp. 23, 127.)

Yes, Christ changes men, and changed men can change the world. Men changed for Christ will be captained by Christ. Like Paul they will be asking, "Lord, what wilt thou have me to do?" (Acts 9:6.) Peter stated they will "follow his steps." (1 Peter 2:21.) John said they will "walk, even as he walked." (1 John 2:6.)

Finally, men captained by Christ will be consumed in Christ. To paraphrase President Harold B. Lee, they set fire in others because they are on fire. (*Stand Ye in Holy Places*, p. 192.)

Their will is swallowed up in his will. (See John 5:30.) They do always those things that please the Lord. (See John 8:29.) Not only would they die for the Lord, but more important they want to live for Him.

Enter their homes, and the pictures on their walls, the books on their shelves, the music in the air, their words and acts reveal them as Christians. They stand as witnesses of God at all times, and in all things, and in all places. (See Mosiah 18:9.) They have Christ on their minds, as they look unto Him in every thought. (See D&C 6:36.) They have Christ in their hearts as their affections are placed on Him forever. (See Alma 37:36.)

Almost every week they partake of the sacrament and witness anew to their Eternal Father that they are willing to take upon them the name of His Son, always remember Him, and keep His commandments. (See Moroni 4:3.)

In Book of Mormon language, they "feast upon the words of Christ" (2 Nephi 32:3), "talk of Christ" (2 Nephi 25:26), "rejoice in Christ" (2 Nephi 25:26), "are made alive in Christ" (2 Nephi 25:25), and "glory in [their] Jesus" (see 2 Nephi 33:6). In short, they lose themselves in the Lord, and find eternal life. (See Luke 17:33.)

President David O. McKay tells of a singular event that happened to him. After falling asleep, he said he "beheld in vision something infinitely sublime." He saw a beautiful city, a great concourse of people dressed in white, and the Savior.

"The city, I understood, was his. It was the City Eternal; and the people following him were to abide there in peace and eternal happiness.

"But who were they?

"As if the Savior read my thoughts, he answered by

pointing to a semicircle that then appeared above them, and on which were written in gold the words:

"These Are They Who Have Overcome the World—Who Have Truly Been Born Again!

"When I awoke, it was breaking day." (*Cherished Experiences from the Writings of President David O. McKay,* pp. 101–2.)

When we awake and are born of God, a new day will break and Zion will be redeemed.

May we be convinced that Jesus is the Christ, choose to follow Him, be changed for Him, captained by Him, consumed in Him, and born again.

Chapter 10

Worthy Fathers, Worthy Sons

The Book of Mormon was meant for us. It was written for our day. Its scriptures are to be likened unto ourselves. (See 1 Nephi 19:23.)

With that understanding, let us consider from the Book of Mormon the responsibility fathers have to teach their sons, and the responsibility sons have to take direction from their fathers. This counsel also applies to all parents and their children.

The opening lines of the Book of Mormon read: "I, Nephi, having been born of goodly parents, therefore I was taught somewhat in all the learning of my father." (1 Nephi 1:1.)

Good fathers teach their sons, and good sons listen and obey. Teaching is done by precept and example, and by word and deed. A good model is the best teacher. Therefore, a father's first responsibility is to set the proper example.

Lehi, Nephi's father, lived an exemplary life. He had a vision in which he "beheld a tree, whose fruit was desirable to make one happy." (1 Nephi 8:10.) This tree represented the love of God. (See 1 Nephi 11:25.) Lehi partook of its fruit, which "filled [his] soul with exceedingly great joy." (1 Nephi 8:12.) After he had a personal testimony of its goodness, he took the next step of inviting his family to also partake.

Here is a divine pattern: As the leader of the family, Lehi first taught by example. He led out in righteousness — in conversion to Christ. Then he taught by word, saying, "Believe as I believe."

What then was Nephi's responsibility after receiving this kind of direction from his father? The Book of Mormon states that Nephi, having heard all the words of his father concerning the things which he saw in vision, was desirous that he might "know of these things, by the power of the Holy Ghost, which is the gift of God unto all those who diligently seek him." (1 Nephi 10:17.)

Nephi had listened to his father, had believed his father, but he wanted to know through the same source his father knew — revelation. Worthy sons are entitled to receive from their Heavenly Father confirmation concerning the direction their mortal fathers give them. It takes revelation to perceive revelation. So Nephi diligently sought the Lord and received a revelation which reaffirmed the revelation his father had given to the family.

What did the righteous fathers of the Book of Mormon teach their sons? They taught them many things, but the overarching message was "the great plan of the Eternal God" — the Fall, rebirth, Atonement, Resurrection, Judgment, eternal life. (See Alma 34:9.) Enos said he knew his father was a just man, "for he taught me in his language, and also in the nurture and admonition of the Lord — and blessed be the name of my God for it." (Enos 1:1.)

Those in the Book of Mormon who were taught nothing concerning the Lord but only concerning worldly knowledge became a cunning and wicked people. (See Mosiah 24:5, 7.)

All truths are not of the same value. The saving truths of salvation are of greatest worth. These truths the fathers taught plainly, frequently, and fervently. Are we doing likewise?

Lehi taught his son Jacob about the sacrifice of the Messiah and the need for "a broken heart and a contrite spirit." He told his son that there is "opposition in all things" and that men are "free to choose liberty and eternal life" through the Lord or "captivity and death" through the devil, who desires all men to "be miserable like unto himself." (2 Nephi 2:7, 11, 27.)

Repetition is a key to learning. Our children need to hear the truth repeated, especially because there is so much falsehood abroad. Devoted Book of Mormon fathers constantly reminded their sons of saving truths. "O remember, remember, my sons, the words which king Benjamin spake unto his people," said Helaman. "Yea, remember that there is no other way nor means whereby man can be saved, only through the atoning blood of Jesus Christ." (Helaman 5:9.) "My sons, remember, remember," Helaman continued, "that it is upon the rock of our Redeemer, who is Christ, the son of God, that ye must build your foundation." (Helaman 5:12.)

In the Book of Mormon, faithful fathers constantly bore their testimonies to their sons. "Remember that these sayings are true, and also that these records are true," King Benjamin testified to his sons. (Mosiah 1:6.) Alma bore witness to his son Helaman saying, "I do know; and the knowledge which I have is of God." (Alma 36:26.)

Great family legacies are kept alive in the Book of Mormon. Alma taught Helaman about how he had heard Helaman's grandfather prophesy. (See Alma 36:17.)

King Benjamin caused that his three sons "should be taught in all the language of his fathers." (Mosiah 1:2.) They needed to understand and use the language of holy writ. If they didn't know the right words, they wouldn't know the plan. The Mulekites had no scriptures, and their language and faith became corrupted. (See Omni 1:17.)

In the Book of Mormon, loving fathers commended their sons when they deserved it. Alma complimented Shiblon, saying, "You have commenced in your youth to look to the Lord." (Alma 38:2.) Mormon told his son Moroni, "I recommend thee unto God." (Moroni 9:22.) Our sons need to be encouraged in their righteous endeavors.

If their sons strayed, stalwart Book of Mormon fathers still continued to teach them. Lehi exhorted two wayward sons with "all the feeling of a tender parent, that they would hearken to his words." (1 Nephi 8:37.) He preached to them and bade them keep the commandments of God. (See 1 Nephi 8:37–38.)

Alma reproved his son Corianton for his immoral behavior. This loving father said it was no excuse that many others were also guilty. (See Alma 39:4.) Alma told Corianton frankly that his conduct made it so that some people would not believe Alma's words. (See Alma 39:11.) Alma then taught him the principle that "wickedness never was happiness." (Alma 41:10.)

Why did righteous fathers in the Book of Mormon go to so much trouble to teach their sons the word of God? King Benjamin said it was to fulfill the commandments of God. (See Mosiah 1:4.) He further stated that were it not for their having the brass plates which contained the commandments, they would have "suffered in ignorance." (Mosiah 1:3.) Could the lack of teaching the scriptures in our homes be a source of our suffering in ignorance today?

As the brass plates blessed Lehi and his descendants, so our scriptures should bless us. "And now, my sons," said King Benjamin, "I would that ye should remember to search them diligently, that ye may profit thereby; and I would that ye should keep the commandments of God." (Mosiah 1:7.) In other words, first read them, then heed them.

At what age do we begin teaching our children these gospel truths? Alma taught his son Helaman while he was in his youth. (See Alma 36:3.) Our youth ought not to wait until the mission field to get a grasp of the scriptures and a closeness to the Lord. Lehi said that his son Jacob beheld the glory of the Lord in his youth. (See 2 Nephi 2:4.) Imagine what would happen to missionary work if we sent out that kind of young men.

How often should fathers teach these truths to their sons? King Benjamin speaks of having the commandments "always before our eyes." (Mosiah 1:5.)

Enos describes the beginning of a great spiritual experience that happened to him this way: "Behold, I went to hunt beasts in the forests; and the words which I had often heard my father speak concerning eternal life, and the joy of the saints, sunk deep into my heart." (Enos 1:3.) Note the phrase "I had often heard my father speak."

In summary, the Book of Mormon, which is the most correct book on earth, demonstrates that the major responsibility for teaching our sons the great plan of the Eternal Father—the Fall, rebirth, Atonement, Resurrection, Judgment, eternal life—rests with fathers. It should be done individually as well as in the family. It should be preached and discussed so our children will know the commandments. It should be done from their youth up — and often.

May we teach our children as the exemplary Book of Mormon fathers taught their sons. And may they, like Nephi, listen and obey, knowing that because of those teachings they too were born of goodly parents.

Chapter 11

Cleansing the Inner Vessel

As I have sought direction from the Lord, I have had reaffirmed in my mind and heart the declaration of the Lord to "say nothing but repentance unto this generation." (D&C 6:9; 11:9.) This has been a theme of every latter-day prophet, along with their testimony that Jesus is the Christ and that Joseph Smith is a prophet of God.

Repentance was the cry of our great prophet, Spencer W. Kimball. This theme permeated his talks and the pages of his writings, such as his marvelous book *The Miracle of Forgiveness*. And it must be our cry today, both to member and to nonmember alike—repent.

Watchmen—what of the night? We must respond by saying that all is not well in Zion. As Captain Moroni counseled, we must cleanse the inner vessel (see Alma 60:23), beginning first with ourselves, then with our families, and finally with the Church.

A prophet of God stated, "Ye shall clear away the bad according as the good shall grow . . . until the good shall overcome the bad." (Jacob 5:66.) It takes a Zion people to make a Zion society, and we must prepare for that.

During the past few years a number of resources have been set in place in the Church to help us. New editions of the scriptures have been published—are we taking advantage of them? More temples are located closer to our people—are we going to the house of the Lord more frequently? The consolidated meeting schedule was set up—are we taking advantage of the increased time with our families? A special home evening manual was provided—are we using it? A new hymnal has just been published—are we singing more songs of the heart? (See D&C 25:12.) And so the list goes on and on. We don't need changed programs now as much as we need changed people.

We remember our beloved President Kimball for many marvelous words of counsel, among which was his encouragement to "lengthen our stride." We needed that direction, for the Book of Mormon warns us of the tactics of the adversary in the last day: "And others will he pacify, and lull them away into carnal security, that they will say: All is well in Zion; yea, Zion prospereth, all is well—and thus the devil cheateth their souls, and leadeth them away carefully down to hell." (2 Nephi 28:21.)

There are many "awake" passages in the Book of Mormon, such as: "O that ye would awake; awake from a deep sleep, yea, even from the sleep of hell . . . awake . . . [and] put on the armor of righteousness. Shake off the chains with which ye are bound, and come forth out of obscurity, and arise from the dust." (2 Nephi 1:13, 23.) As a people, it seems we can survive persecution easier and better than we can peace and prosperity.

The plaguing sin of this generation is sexual immorality. This, the Prophet Joseph said, would be the source of more temptations, more buffetings, and more difficulties for the elders of Israel than any other. (See *Journal of Discourses* 8:55.)

President Joseph F. Smith said that sexual impurity

would be one of the three dangers that would threaten the Church within—and so it does. (See *Gospel Doctrine,* pp. 312–13.) It permeates our society.

In the category of sins, the Book of Mormon places unchastity next to murder. (See Alma 39:5.) As Alma states, "Now . . . I would that ye should repent and forsake your sins, and go no more after the lusts of your eyes, . . . for except ye do this ye can in nowise inherit the kingdom of God." (Alma 39:9.) If we are to cleanse the inner vessel, we must forsake immorality and be clean.

Unless we read the Book of Mormon and give heed to its teachings, the Lord has stated in section 84 of the Doctrine and Covenants that the whole Church is under condemnation: "And this condemnation resteth upon the children of Zion, even all." (D&C 84:56.) The Lord continues: "And they shall remain under this condemnation until they repent and remember the new covenant, even the Book of Mormon and the former commandments which I have given them, not only to say, but to do according to that which I have written." (D&C 84:57.)

Now we not only need to *say* more about the Book of Mormon, but we need to *do* more with it. Why? The Lord answers: "That they may bring forth fruit meet for their Father's kingdom; otherwise there remaineth a scourge and judgment to be poured out upon the children of Zion." (D&C 84:58.) We have felt that scourge and judgment!

The Prophet Joseph said that "the Book of Mormon was the most correct of any book on earth, and the keystone of our religion, and a man would get nearer to God by abiding by its precepts, than any other book." The Book of Mormon has not been, nor is it yet, the center of our personal study, family teaching, preaching, and missionary work. Of this we must repent. I do not know of a man who has been more true to the Book of Mormon than President Marion G. Romney. In a general conference address, he declared that the Book of Mormon was "the most effective piece of missionary literature we have." He quoted the Doctrine and Covenants, which states that "the Book of Mormon and the holy scriptures are given of me for your instruction" (D&C 33:16), and that "the elders, priests and teachers of this church shall teach the principles of my gospel, which are in the Bible and the Book of Mormon" (D&C 42:12). President Romney added, "It is of course obvious that unless we read, study, and learn the principles which are in the Book of Mormon, we, the elders, priests, and teachers of 'this church,' cannot comply with this direction to teach them.

"But there is another reason why we should read it," President Romney continued. "By doing so we will fill and refresh our minds with the constant flow of that 'water' which Jesus said would be in us — 'a well of water springing up into everlasting life.' (John 4:14.) We must obtain a continuing supply of this water if we are to resist evil and retain the blessings of being born again. . . .

"If we would avoid adopting the evils of the world, we must pursue a course which will daily feed our minds with and call them back to the things of the Spirit. I know of no better way to do this than by reading the Book of Mormon."

And then he concluded: "And so, I counsel you, my beloved brothers and sisters and friends everywhere, to make reading in the Book of Mormon a few minutes each day a lifelong practice. . . . I feel certain that if, in our homes, parents will read from the Book of Mormon prayerfully and regularly, both by themselves and with their children, the spirit of that great book will come to permeate our homes and all who dwell therein. The spirit of reverence will increase; mutual respect and consideration for each other will grow. The spirit of contention will depart. Parents will counsel their children in greater love and wisdom. Children will be more responsive and submissive to that counsel. Righteousness will increase. Faith, hope, and charity—the pure love of Christ—will abound in our homes and lives, bringing in their wake peace, joy, and happiness." (*Conference Report*, April 1960, pp. 110–13.)

May I now discuss a subject of grave concern that deserves deeper development than we have time. It is the subject of pride.

In the scriptures there is no such thing as righteous pride. It is always considered as a sin. We are not speaking of a wholesome view of self-worth, which is best established by a close relationship with God. But we are speaking of pride as the universal sin, as someone has described it.

Mormon writes that "the pride of this nation, or the people of the Nephites, hath proven their destruction." (Moroni 8:27.) The Lord says in the Doctrine and Covenants, "Beware of pride, lest ye become as the Nephites of old." (D&C 38:39.)

Essentially, pride is a "my will" rather than "thy will" approach to life. The opposite of pride is humbleness, meekness, submissiveness (see Alma 13:28), or teachableness.

In the early days of the restored church, the Lord warned two of its prominent members about pride. To Oliver Cowdery, he said, "Beware of pride, lest thou shouldst enter into temptation." (D&C 23:1.) To Emma Smith, he said, "Continue in the spirit of meekness, and beware of pride." (D&C 25:14.)

"Thou shalt not be proud in thy heart," the Lord warns

us. (D&C 42:40.) "Humble yourselves before God," says the Book of Mormon. (Mosiah 4:10.)

When the earth is cleansed by burning in the last days, the proud shall be as stubble. (See 3 Nephi 25:1; D&C 29:9; 64:24.)

The great and spacious building which Lehi saw was the pride of the world where the multitude of the earth was gathered. (See 1 Nephi 11:35–36.) Those who walked the strait and narrow path and held onto the word of God were mocked and scorned by those in the building. (See 1 Nephi 8:20, 27, 33; 11:25.) "The humble followers of Christ" are few. (2 Nephi 28:14.)

Pride does not look up to God and care about what is right. It looks sideways to man and argues who is right. Pride is manifest in the spirit of contention.

Was it not through pride that the devil became the devil? Christ wanted to serve. The devil wanted to rule. Christ wanted to bring men to where he was. The devil wanted to be above men.

Christ removed self as the force in His perfect life. It was not *my* will, but *thine* be done.

Pride is characterized by "What do I want out of life?" rather than by "What would God have me do with my life?" It is self-will as opposed to God's will. It is the fear of man over the fear of God.

Humility responds to God's will—to the fear of His judgments and to the needs of those around us. To the proud, the applause of the world rings in their ears; to the humble, the applause of heaven warms their hearts.

Someone has said, "Pride gets no pleasure out of having something, only out of having more of it than the next man." Of one brother, the Lord said, "I, the Lord, am not well pleased with him, for he seeketh to excel, and he is not sufficiently meek before me." (D&C 58:41.)

The two groups in the Book of Mormon that seemed to have the greatest difficulty with pride are the "learned, and the rich." (2 Nephi 28:15.) But the word of God can pull down pride. (See Alma 4:19.)

With pride, there are many curses. With humility, there come many blessings. For example, "Be thou humble; and the Lord thy God shall lead thee by the hand, and give thee answer to thy prayers." (D&C 112:10.) The humble will "be made strong, and blessed from on high, and receive knowledge." (D&C 1:28.) The Lord is "merciful unto those who confess their sins with humble hearts." (D&C 61:2.) Humility can turn away God's anger. (See Helaman 11:11.)

As we cleanse the inner vessel, there will have to be changes made in our own personal lives, in our families, and in the Church. The proud do not change to improve, but defend their position by rationalizing. Repentance means change, and it takes a humble person to change. But we can do it.

We have made some wonderful strides in the past. We will be lengthening our stride in the future. To do so, we must first cleanse the inner vessel by awaking and arising, being morally clean, using the Book of Mormon in a manner so that God will lift the condemnation, and finally conquering pride by humbling ourselves.

We can do it. I know we can. That we will do so is my prayer for all of us. God bless you for all the good you have done and will be doing. I leave my blessings on all of you and do so in the name of the Lord Jesus Christ, amen.

Bibliography

Cherished Experiences from the Writings of President David O. McKay. Compiled by Clare Middlemiss. Salt Lake City: Deseret Book Company, 1976.

Hymns of The Church of Jesus Christ of Latter-day Saints. Salt Lake City: Deseret Book Company, 1985.

Journal of Discourses, 26 vols. London: Latter-day Saints' Book Depot, 1854–86.

Lectures on Faith. Salt Lake City: Deseret Book Company, 1985.

Lee, Harold B. *Stand Ye in Holy Places.* Salt Lake City: Deseret Book Company, 1974.

Smith, Joseph, Jr. *History of the Church of Jesus Christ of Latter-day Saints.* Edited by B. H. Roberts. 7 vols. Salt Lake City: The Church of Jesus Christ of Latter-day Saints, 1948. Cited as *History of the Church.*

Smith, Joseph F. *Gospel Doctrine.* Salt Lake City: Deseret Book Company, 1975.

Stepping Stones to an Abundant Life. Compiled by Llewelyn R. McKay. Salt Lake City: Deseret Book Company, 1971.

Index